Cutting peat in Somerset. The large blocks of peat were cut with spades and placed on low-slung barrows to be taken away for 'slitting' into thinner slices that dried more quickly.

INTRODUCTION

For centuries the work of farming was carried out by hand, with tools fashioned in wood or iron, often with considerable ingenuity in fitting the implement for the exact task. Apart from the use of the ox and the horse, man had little to help him in his constant struggle with the elements until the early nineteenth century when machines began to make an impact upon farming methods.

One of the curious things about hand tools, however, is that they survived the onslaught of machine methods and remained in use long after mechanisation had overtaken hand techniques on most of the larger farms.

There are at least two reasons for the continued use of hand implements into our own century. The first is related to the agricultural decline of the 1870s, when ordinary men were faced with the task of providing for large families on a sparse weekly wage. Every farm labourer's family depended upon the plot of allotment which enabled it to eke out a frugal existence. Second, in a situation where labour was cheap, machines like the steam plough were not always competitive. So at both levels of rural society there were practical reasons for the retention of the old hand tools.

Local traditions played a part in determining the precise shape a tool assumed. Time had a hand in altering fashions but it was not as important as geography. Bygones which have survived are not all in museums. They have a habit of turning up in unexpected places and many people have begun to collect these relics of an almost lost technology.

The pages which follow describe examples of some of the hand implements prized by our forefathers.

3

PARING AND BURNING

Before chemicals were introduced the farm-worker had to destroy pests the hard way. The old method involved the removal of a thin layer of topsoil containing the weeds and insect larvae. This was then burnt and reduced to ash which was worked back into the ground. The tool used for this laborious process was the breast plough. The fact that the primitive breast plough survived into the early years of this century demonstrates just how strong, and long, rural traditions once were. This tool is about as simple a device as man can contrive. Shaped like a spade, with one edge fashioned to make a right angle with the rest of the blade, it has a long shaft — a good 6 feet — that is topped by a wide handle.

great effort from the operator — who pushed with the thighs. Protection from the jarring handle was possible if thigh pads, called beaters, were worn. These primitive ploughs were used for many different tasks. H. J. Massingham in 'Country Relics' records how two stalwarts of Cutsdean, Gloucestershire, could plough and burn off an acre of stubble in a day with this crude device. Among other things it was used to cut turf and level molehills. In Devon roadmen used it for drainage ditches. Various parts of England gave it a local name: 'cast cutter' (Kent) and 'velling spade' (Cornwall). Its use on allotments and cottage gardens seems to have persisted long after machines replaced it on the fields.

TOP LEFT:*The shaft of the breast plough is morticed into the handle and the two flanking supports give the handle added strength. In use this cumbersome implement must have exacted*

TOP RIGHT: *Detail of another type of breast plough with a heavier blade. This example comes from the Cotswolds but ploughs of a similar kind were used as far away as Rutland.*

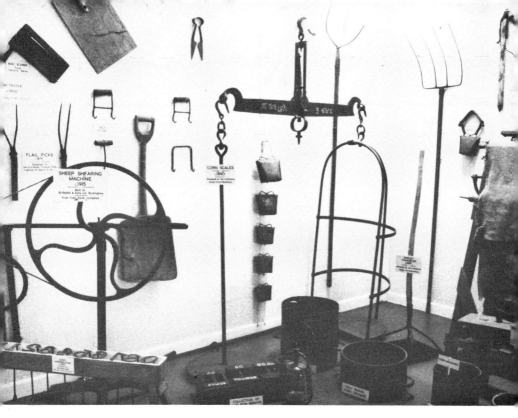

ABOVE: *A selection of tools and other implements which can be seen at the Countryside Museum, Bicton Gardens, East Budleigh, Devon.*

OPPOSITE: *A sower from a nineteenth-century engraving.*

OLD FARM TOOLS

John Vince

Shire Publications Ltd.

CONTENTS

Printed in Great Britain by C. I. Thomas & Sons (Haverfordwest) Ltd, Press Buildings, Merlins Bridge, Haverfordwest.

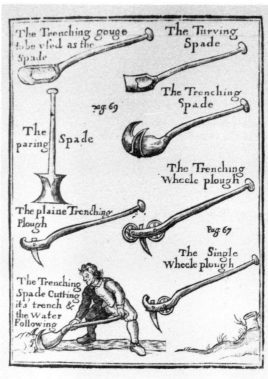

ABOVE: An illustration from a seventeenth-century treatise on agriculture.

DUNG SPREADING

When the soil had been cleaned with the plough and the stubble or the scutch had been burnt the important task of manuring began. Carts were pulled by horse to the midden where the slow and heavy work of loading went on.

RIGHT: *This dung fork is about as simple a tool as you can imagine and its seven joints are pegged together with dowels. From prehistoric times until the nineteenth century such simple tools were made by countrymen too poor, or too prudent, to employ a more expensive tool made with iron.*

BELOW: *A dung drag, used for pulling farmyard manure from the dung cart in the field.*

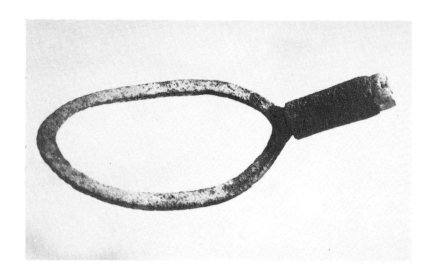

ABOVE: *A muck knocker, used to spread cow pats on the Midland fattening pastures. This very localised tool has a pointed tang which is driven into a long wooden handle; to prevent it splitting, a short iron sleeve, a ferrule, was fitted to the end.*

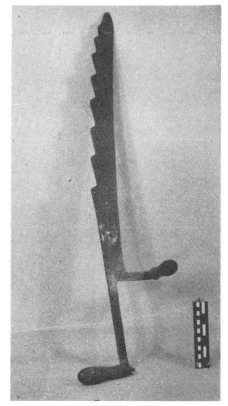

RIGHT: *A mature heap of dung was very solid and compact heaps had to be cut into with a manure knife. This two handed instrument has its handles fixed with wedges. In an 8 hour day one man was supposed to be able to load about 20 cart loads (of about 15 cwt.) and the daily rate of pay was about 3 shillings! The cost of carting was reckoned at one shilling per ton per mile.*

CULTIVATING

One of the fascinating things about farming tools is the way traditional designs have continued almost unchanged. Compare the seventeenth-century sketch and the nineteenth-century illustration shown below. The use, in 1620, of a clotting beetle may be a commentary on the efficiency of ploughing at that time, or it could equally well be a reflection on poor drainage arrangements. The shape of the implement designed for wet clods looks intrinsically weak and it is not surprising to find that it did not apparently survive. The aggressive weeding nippers must have been very effective in practice.

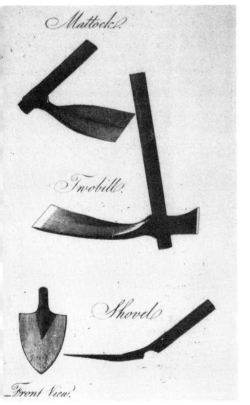

LEFT: A mattock, twobill and a shovel, from Charles Vancouver's 'General View of the Agriculture of the County of Devon' (1808).

BELOW: Implements illustrated in Gervase Markham's 'Farewell to Husbandry' (1620): 1. a hack for breaking clods after ploughing; 2. a clotting beetle for breaking clods after harrowing; 3. a clotting beetle for wet clods; 4. weeding nippers; 5. a paring shovel for clearing ground and destroying weeds.

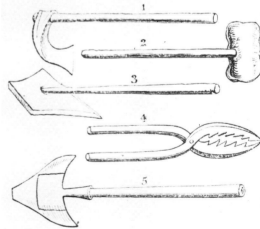

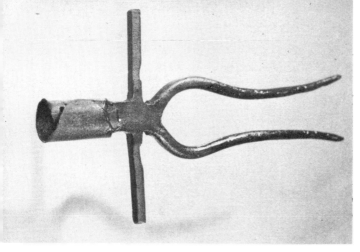

LEFT: *Certain tools have an exotic appearance which may mislead us. The elegantly curved horns, which look as if they belong to an Egyptian deity, on this dock lifter do in fact have a very practical purpose. The cross-piece was provided to allow a foot to persuade the horns to penetrate the soil. With its handle this tool would have been about four feet in length.*

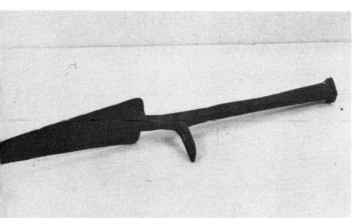

LEFT: *Good drains are laid well below the surface and if a wide-edged tool was employed a lot of soil had to be moved. To save effort and cost, drainage tools were narrow and with them deep gullies could be cut for drainpipes. This drainage spade is made in one piece. The metal shaft made it possible to hammer it into hard ground. At the top the burred edges made by the sledge hammer can still be seen.*

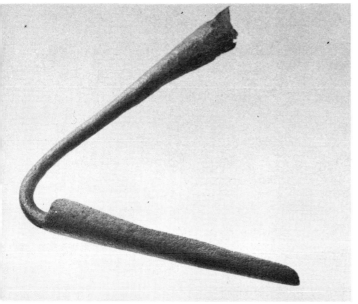

LEFT: *A drainage spade for digging the last spit from the bench. This tool would have had a wooden handle, but the socket is mutilated, and it may well have been modified for some other use such as planting out.*

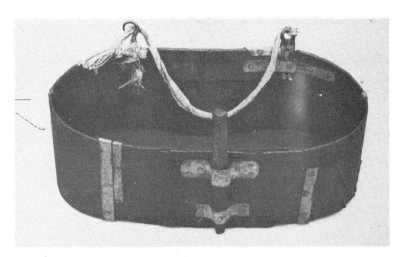

ABOVE: *The prospect of a lonely sower making his way across acres of ploughing broadcasting seed to right and left may conjure up a nostalgic picture of old England but it was a dreadfully inefficient method even though it persisted for thousands of years. A sower carried his seed in a seed-lip like the one shown here. This one has a handle so that the sower could hold it steady.*
BELOW LEFT: *From the length of the handles of* these robust weeding tongs we may judge that they could administer a good nip.
BELOW RIGHT: *Stones were troublesome to the ploughman and a good deal of effort was made to clear them from the fields. Children and women provided most of the labour. They made use of small stone rakes like this one. The heaps of stones collected were carted away to repair the roads.*

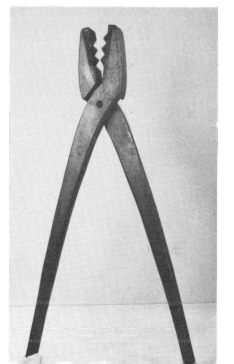

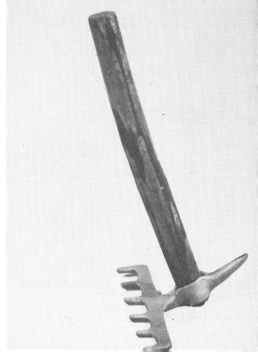

OPPOSITE TOP LEFT: *One of the farm labourer's most important domestic crops was the potato. Once these had been sown the next task was to mould them up with a hoe or a ridging tool. This device, with its semi-circular blade, was worked between rows and made half a mound for each row as it went along. For work in the fields a potato plough was also used but the result was just the same.*

OPPOSITE TOP RIGHT: *The crop was bagged with the aid of a potato shovel. This kind of implement can still be found in use in the potato country of Lincolnshire. The bell-shaped shovel has a wide lip that is robust enough to penetrate the soil but its main function is to gather as many tubers as possible. The rods which form the basket-like interior are riveted at each end. Surplus soil falls through the spaces.*

OPPOSITE BOTTOM LEFT: *This potato planter made a round hole at the required depth. The*

cross-piece served the same purpose as the upper edge of a fork or shovel.

OPPOSITE BOTTOM RIGHT: *A potato planter with a device to adjust the width of the hole.*

ABOVE: *A wooden spade for digging clay. In use it must have been a very heavy tool to handle.*

BELOW: *In some parts of England the heavy clay soil was worked with this iron tool, a cross between a spade and a fork. The metal implement was probably more efficient for digging clay as its sparse surface provided less resistance. Tools of this kind, with or without a central prong, were made by the blacksmith who no doubt followed local tradition. It is easy to forget that at the end of the last century, when conditions in rural England were quite severe, the countryman often took his open spade out into the October moonlight in order to prepare his own allotment.*

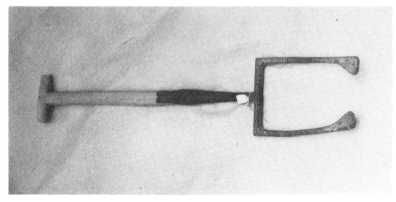

RIGHT: *The prized boots purchased with the extra money earned at harvest time could become badly worn with digging, so the prudent man used a spade iron. This fitted the sole of the boot and the lip at the rear protected the wearer's heel. The iron was held in position by a lace which was threaded through the two eyelets in the sidestraps.*

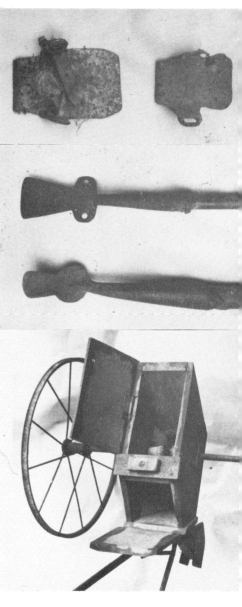

RIGHT: *The farmer waged a constant battle against weeds. As he walked about his farm he poked up any offending plant with the paddle that was attached to the end of his stick. There are several designs to be found but one of the most attractive is the symbolic thistle shaped variety.*

BELOW: *Not all seeds were sown with horse drawn drills: small manual seed barrows were numerous. These wheels are adjustable on the axle and their distance apart was determined by the kind of seed being sown. A coulter at the front made a drill for the expelled seed.*

ABOVE: *A view inside the seed barrow hopper. A circular brush, like a miniature sweep's, was fixed to the axle. As the barrow moved the brush rotated and carried seeds upwards so that they could drop into the funnel at the rear and into the drill made by the coulter.*

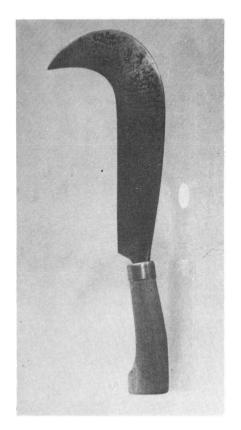 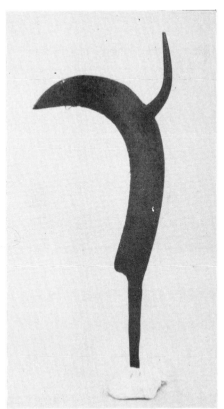

HEDGES AND FENCES

The English landscape assumed its present appearance, with hedges bounding often irregular shaped fields, in the eighteenth century. These kept cattle on the grazing land and gave arable crops the maximum protection. There were hedgerows before the eighteenth century of course; and some aouble hedges, which may define boundaries as old as Saxon times, clearly have a great antiquity.

The hedger's basic tool is the billhook and this humble implement has taken on various shapes. In the Tower of London are the an-

cestral outlines of those illustrated here. The billhook is a kin to the weapons of the middle ages. The billhook on a longer shaft became a battle-axe and the smiths who went to war took with them their own traditions of design.

ABOVE LEFT: *A billhook made at Bramley, Hants.*

ABOVE RIGHT: *An alternative design with an extra spike which could be used as a lever.*

RIGHT: *Wire fences became popular in the nineteenth century. To stretch the wire tightly between the iron posts the wire strainer was invented. This example has a screw thread.*

BELOW LEFT: *An alternative type of wire strainer which was worked by the long lever and a ratchet mechanism.*

BELOW RIGHT: *This device, which is really a form of drill, was used to bore holes for fence posts.*

LIVESTOCK

The development of root crops and all the other changes which took place in agriculture in the eighteenth century enabled farmers to keep stock alive during the long cold winter months. This was a great improvement as it helped to ensure a supply of fresh meat throughout the year instead of salted beef during the winter.

BELOW LEFT: *Many farmers treated their own sick animals. These are the essential tools used for bleeding creatures suffering from blood pressure. The vein was severed with one of the blades of the fleam (this example has three blades). An old farming manual provides us with a description of the method — 'raise the jugular vein on the right side by pressing it with* the fingers, hold the fleam in the left hand parallel with the vein, and give it a smart blow with the blood stick; keep the bucket pressed against the neck below the wound, and if the blood does not flow freely insert the fingers in the mouth to keep the jaw moving. Take from 1 to 3 quarts of blood, afterwards place a pin through the lips of the wound and wind tow around it. Do not use too large a fleam'. The fleam for cattle was larger than the one used on horses. The blood stick was made of wood.

BELOW RIGHT: *This curious device was probably used to hold an animal's head in position during treatment.*

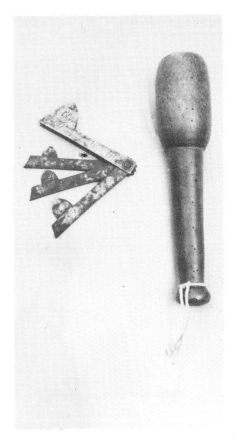

OPPOSITE: *A selection of cheese making equipment from the dairy exhibit at the Countryside Museum, Bicton Gardens, East Budleigh, Devon.*

LEFT: *This pestle and mortar were used by a farmer who mixed his own medicines.*

BELOW LEFT: *To keep an animal still during treatment was not easy. The thongs on these 'twists' were wrapped round the tongue and twisted tight. The method was crude but effective.*

BELOW RIGHT: *Once the pills had been made the animal had to be persuaded to take them. With this dispenser, which is really a kind of blow pipe, the tablet could be shot into the animal's throat.*

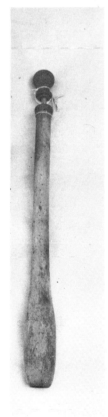

16

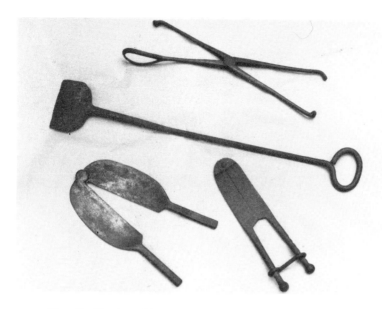

ABOVE:*The tails of lambs and horses were often removed, or docked, when they were young. This process was brief but painful. Docking irons look like shears but the pivot is at the top of the blade. A pocket knife was often a substitute when lambs were docked. After the removal of the tail the wound was usually seared with the red hot searing iron (centre) which reduced the bleeding and helped to prevent infection. The lambing forceps (top) were patented in 1895.*

BELOW: *Draughts were administered with drenching horns like the ones shown here.*

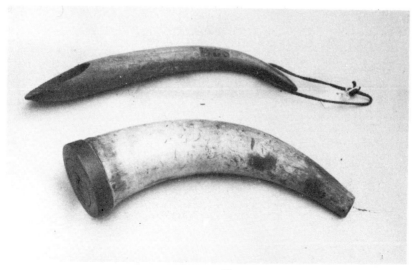

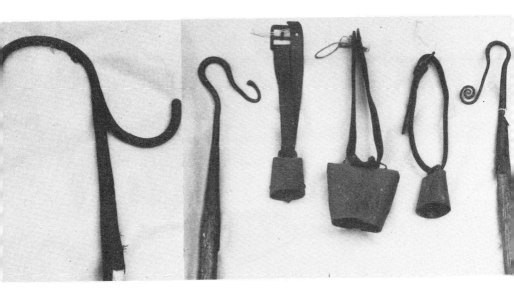

TOP LEFT: *This variation on the traditional shepherd's crook (a dipping hook) was used to push the sheep down into the water when they were dipped. One half could be used to hold the sheep's head out of the water.*

TOP RIGHT: *Sheep-bells were used in the days before fenced fields. The bell was sometimes attached to the sheep's neck with a small wooden yoke that held two looped straps but dog-collar straps were also used. To improve the tone of a bell it was often given a coat of brass and old bells frequently have a patchy look as the brass did not usually adhere or wear evenly. These bells and crooks were once used on the Cotswolds.*

RIGHT: *Shearing time, in June, was a busy season for the shepherd. In the old days teams of shearers led by their captain could be seen trudging the dusty roads, passing from one farm to another. These sheep shears are not as old as their case which bears the name 'Robert Cook 1779' on one side and 'I. S. 1844' on the other. Perhaps the case was handed down by the original owner.*

HAYTIME

Between seedtime and harvest the farmer had to attend to the hay which was essential for winter feed. The hay was cut and then gathered with rakes.

ABOVE: *This drag rake (also called a heel rake or a dew rake in some places) has a split willow handle. Its twin ends fit into the oak stock which holds the ash tines. In use the tines are moved parallel to the ground. With the drag rake the hay was gathered into lines (called*

windrows) so that men with pitchforks could load the haycart without taking any unnecessary steps.

BELOW: *When hay was made into trusses it was bound together with hay bonds. These were twisted together with the wimble, in about ten seconds or so. Hay sold between 1st June and 31st August was called new hay and had to weigh 60 lbs per truss. Any hay sold from September to June was old hay and had to weigh 56 lbs per truss.*

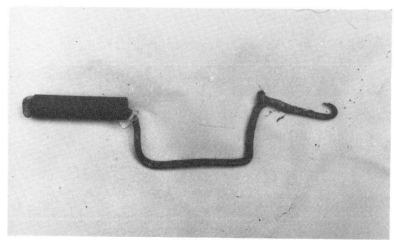

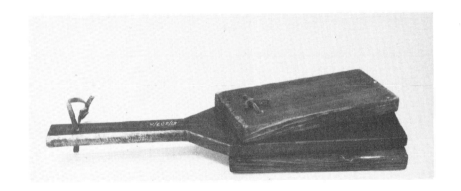

BIRD STARVING

Once the grain was sown it needed watching to keep the birds away. This work was usually undertaken by children — who were not obliged to attend school at all until the 1880 Education Act. The bird scarer's day was a long one — from sunrise to sunset. Various things were used to make a suitable noise to scare away the birds.

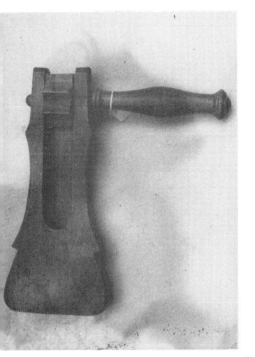

ABOVE: *One of the simplest contraptions was a small wooden bat with a clapper attached to each side by a leather thong. This crude arrangement effectively generated enough noise when waved up and down.*

LEFT: *Another kind of bird scarer has now found a new role — among football supporters. The rattle is clearly the proto-type for those known to the F. A. Two thin strips of wood are arranged to click over the teeth of the two cogs which are fixed to the spindle held by the handle. The larger board to which the strips are fixed serves as a sounding board and a kind of fly-wheel to maintain the motion provided by the user. The example shown seems to be the work of a skilled carpenter as it bears several refinements and a fine finish.*

TOP LEFT: *Pseudo-animate scarers like this were usually placed on the ground and held there with a metal rod that was slipped into the holes arranged in the two small brackets on the reverse side. This specimen may also have been suspended in a tree by the two holes, at the apex of its back. Objects of this sort perhaps added a little relief to the blacksmith's usual work and* enabled him to display his hidden talents.

TOP RIGHT: *The ends of the fork of this clapper were flattened and punched to allow a rod to be fixed between. The loose metal discs banged together to make the noise. The discs have uncomfortable looking edges but squares were easier to cut than circles.*

LEFT: *This more sophisticated bird scarer takes the form of a hawk, designed to be suspended from a wire like a mobile. From the appearance of the wings and body this figure has an unmistakable factory-made look. It is made from pressed sheet that was shaped on a die.*

HARVEST

Cutting the ripe corn, or reaping, was done with a sickle or a scythe. Women seem to have used the sickle right up to this century in various parts of England. An alternative to the sickle — a teethed hewk — was employed in the north of England and, although the hewk was difficult to use, once the technique had been mastered it was a more efficient implement. Its blade was narrower than the conventional sickle and throughout the length of its cutting edge was a line of fine saw-like teeth. In use it was unlike a sickle as the reaper had to grasp the stalks with the left hand so that their collective bulk could offer enough resistance to the swinging blade, which required very little sharpening. Reapers at work with the hewk were said to be 'hand shearing' in contrast to those who would be 'striking' with a sickle. A sickle could cut more at each stroke and the reaper had an armful to set down for the bindster who followed. Hand shearing was claimed to be superior nevertheless as no time was wasted in sharpening.

The advantage of using a scythe was speed. Between three-quarters and one acre of corn or hay could be cut per man per day compared with a mere quarter of an acre with a sickle. Scythes vary in the way the batt (handle) is shaped.

There are four parts to a scythe: the blade, the shaft (variously known as snead, snaith or batt), the two adjustable handles (known as doles, hand-pins or nibs), and at the junction of the blade and batt there is always a gap protected by a thin wire or rod called a grass nail. This had an important part to play as it prevented the tool from becoming choked with stalks that had been mown.

RIGHT: *A scythe with a batt that is almost straight. The grass nail is missing although the hole it fitted into can be seen.*

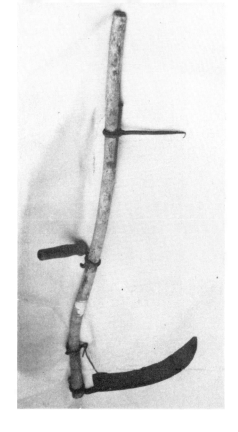

LEFT: *This scythe has a very short blade and it was probably used for cutting bracken.*

BOTTOM RIGHT: *It was essential to have a keen edged tool when mowing and the scythe was 'whetted' as occasion demanded with a strickle. This device (called a "ripe stick" in Wales) was a square piece of oak with a rounded handle. The squared section was pitted like the surface of a file. A strickle was not much use on its own and a mixture of grease (mutton fat) and sand was smeared across its surface before the scythe's edge could be rubbed.*

BOTTOM LEFT: *The horn of a cow (a strickle horn) was used to carry the essential ointment. Soft sand was used for hay, sharp sand for corn and small pebbles for bramble and bracken. The rougher the task the rougher the edge had to be. It is easy to confuse a strickle horn with a drenching horn — see page 18.*

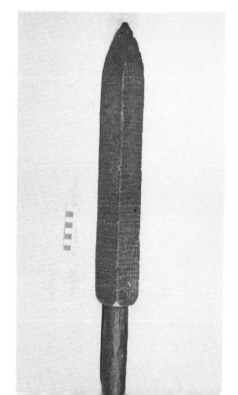

LEFT: *There were various hook-shaped tools employed on the land but they all served different purposes. 1: Reaping hook. 2: Sickle with a toothed blade. 3: A turnip knife. 4: Bill hook used for hedging.*

BOTTOM LEFT: *Pick thanks were held in the left hand. These simple hooks gathered the standing corn into a sheaf ready for the swish of the sickle.*

BOTTOM RIGHT: *An apple hook, used to bring the fruit within reach for picking.*

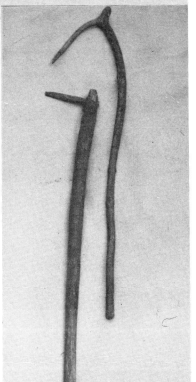

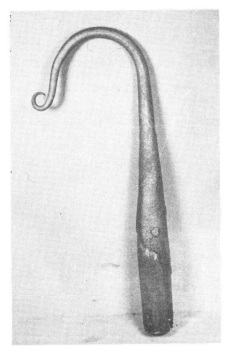

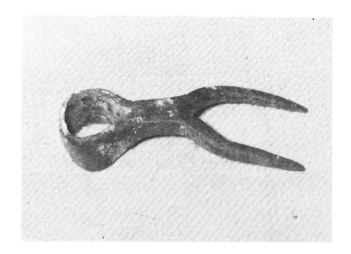

PEAT CUTTING

Long before coal became a common domestic fuel most fires were kept going with wood alone. The right to collect fuel from the forest was as ancient as the village itself. Not all parts of England were equally well endowed with timber and where it was not available peat was burnt instead.

Peat is very much younger than coal in the geological time scale and the peat bogs we see today began to form in about 7000 B.C. In the natural cycle of events dead vegetable matter decomposes and its constituent chemicals are subjected to the various changes which cause the fibrous structure to break up. Where this cycle did not follow the usual pattern peat bogs formed. The bacteria which caused decay failed to mature in a waterlogged soil and a climate that became too cool to sustain them. The progression of seasons throughout many centuries caused the layer of vegetable matter to thicken steadily. Man began to exploit this useful source of fuel and different kinds of tools and equipment were designed for its extraction.

Peat is to be found in widely scattered parts of the British Isles, such as Somerset, Norfolk and the Isle of Lewis. On Lewis the peat cutting is a collective affair and neighbour aids neighbour in cutting, carting and stacking. Peat is often cut far across the moor and when it is dried it has to be carried to the nearest roadway where it is stacked ready for collection. A basket strapped to the back is the common method of carrying in the Hebrides and this task usually falls upon the womenfolk. The baskets are known as 'kreels'.

Peat is methodically cut in banks and one year's cutting begins where the last year's ended. In this way the landscape has slowly undergone a gentle change in its contours. A peat iron or knife can look like a small spade and in Scotland it usually has an angled edge—rather like the breast plough. Each slice of peat is left to dry out before it is collected for stacking.

A single peat — about a foot long and eight inches wide — seems as light as a feather. It is a curious thing to see along the village, peat in neat stacks placed as close to the cottage door as possible, and to see a howling gale fail to dislodge even one. The art lies in the stacking of course and spaces are left so that the wind can blow through a stack from almost any direction.

LEFT: *A peat basket which was carried on the back. In the Hebrides it is known as a kreel and is traditionally used by women.*

BOTTOM LEFT: *A peat knife from Devon. Notice the upturned edge which is similar but smaller to the breast plough shown on page 4.*

BOTTOM RIGHT: *A Cornish peat knife with a flat blade.*

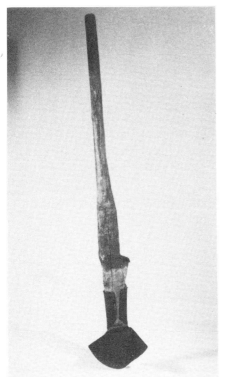

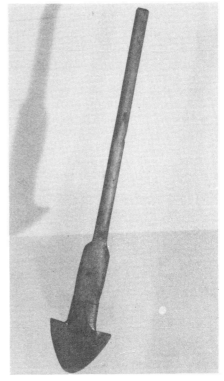

MISCELLANEOUS TOOLS

There are many ancient tools which present the collector with a puzzle. A few of these are shown here but it would not be difficult to fill a whole book with them.

CENTRE: *This unusual tool was often to be found in the barns or store sheds. It was used to grip the heavy hessian sacks when they had to* be loaded into the farmer's market cart. You can still find the odd sack hook in the country curio shop.

BOTTOM: *Two men were needed to carry a sack if it was placed on this sack carrier. Such things were made by the village carpenter. There were no sharp parts to splinter and tear the sacks as all the edges were carefully rounded.*

ABOVE LEFT: *Although eels are not a uniformly popular form of food they were considered differently in the harder days of the last century. Many water-millers sported an eel trap on their sluices. But the alternative to the eel trap was the eel spear which took upon itself a variety of designs.*

A good many eels were probably transfixed by this barbed device. It is a good example of

blacksmith's work and shows us just how skilled the village craftsmen were.

ABOVE RIGHT: *This is another eel spear. Carefully arranged prongs provided a narrowing range of teeth designed to hold even the squirmiest eel in place. However good the spear was the hunter needed to have a quick eye and a fast reaction to secure his catch.*

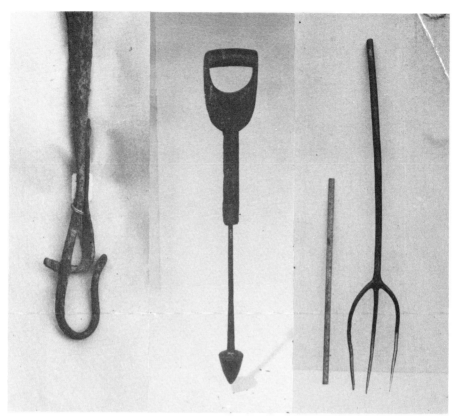

LEFT: *A spring hook used for well buckets.*
CENTRE: *A dibble for making the holes in which seeds were sown. The labourer held a dibble in each hand and walked backwards making holes about eight inches apart. The wife or children followed, placing seeds in the holes.*

RIGHT: *An ash-wood barley fork used for turning mown barley in the field.*
BELOW: *With this unusual hoe two rows could be worked at a time. The open design of this tool helped to give it the title 'look crook' in Yorkshire.*

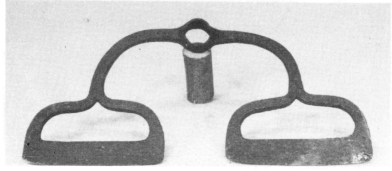

LEFT: *Before strings came into use, in the late nineteenth century, hops were grown on a 'hill' of three or five poles. A hop dog like this was used to lever up the poles. The same name was also given to the long handled knife with its curled end used for hoisting the hops up and off the pole.*

BELOW LEFT: *1: a rat trap; 2: a mouse trap; 3: a pole trap which was attached to the top of a favourite perch and caught a bird when it landed. Pole traps are now illegal.*

BELOW RIGHT: *A knife used for chopping the leaves off turnips. The spike at the end enabled the labourer to pick up each root without bending.*

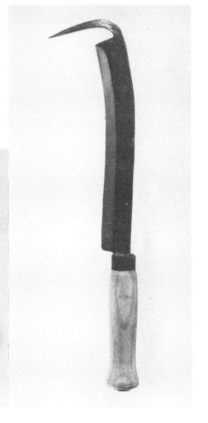